BEAT THE BILL COLLECTOR

BEAT THE BILL COLLECTOR

How to Obtain
Freedom from Your Debt

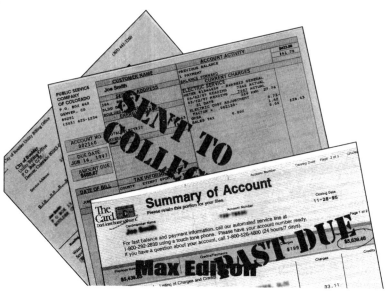

PALADIN PRESS • BOULDER, COLORADO

Beat the Bill Collector: How to Obtain Freedom from Your Debt
by Max Edison

Copyright © 1997 by Max Edison

ISBN 0-87364-949-4
Printed in the United States of America

Published by Paladin Press, a division of
Paladin Enterprises, Inc., P.O. Box 1307,
Boulder, Colorado 80306, USA.
(303) 443-7250

Direct inquiries and/or orders to the above address.

PALADIN, PALADIN PRESS, and the "horse head" design
are trademarks belonging to Paladin Enterprises and
registered in United States Patent and Trademark Office.

Contents

Warning

The author, publisher, and distributors of this book do not advocate any illegal actions, nor are they engaged in rendering legal service or advice. The services of a professional are recommended if legal advice or assistance is needed. The author, publisher, and distributors of this book disclaim any responsibility for personal loss or liability caused by the use or misuse of any information presented herein. This book is *for information purposes only.*

Disclaimer

I hate like heck to even have to write this, as it kind of insinuates that someone I tried to help might think about suing me, but in today's litigous society you've got to do these things or the shysters will start chewing on your leg like a pack of rabid wombats.

The information you're about to read is not legal advice in the strictest sense. It's advice, sure, and it's about the law, but I'm no lawyer. If I was, I'd be charging you $50 to $100 an hour rather than whatever ridiculously low price you paid for this book. The information in this book is accurate and current, to the best of my knowledge, but you just never know what'll happen, so if you follow the advice, *you do so at your own risk.* Think of me as your next-door neighbor, co-worker, or cousin—somebody who's been through experiences of the kind you're having now. Just don't think of me as your lawyer.

Preface

Welcome to the seamy world of collection agencies, where people are guilty until proven innocent and customer service has an all-new meaning. I trust your stay will be a profitable one. This is a book about how to skip out on money you owe, or at least to put off paying it until your circumstances are better. While I would generally advise you to pay what you owe, both for your credit and your peace of mind, you are free to do whatever you wish with this information. Remember (again) that I'm not your lawyer, and that no rule applies to all situations.

As far as I know, this is the only book about collection agencies currently in print. Bill collectors have a sort of unwritten rule of *omerta*, or code of silence, similar to that of cops and mafiosi. New collection strategies or humorous stories about work circulate between collectors but don't generally get out into public. As a result, the public fights a losing battle when collectors call.

There is, I think, a stigma in getting collection calls and notices in today's America, but there really shouldn't be. Most people go through collections proceedings at one time or another: in college, at times when business is slow, when laid off or unemployed, and even when refusing to pay a disputed account. When I worked at Aggressive Agencies, a collection agency in Minneapolis, I collected (or tried to collect) money from doctors, lawyers, ministers, bricklayers, business owners, soldiers, and the clinically insane. Collections agencies are the great equalizer, the ugly underbelly of a credit-driven society.

In the next six chapters, you'll find the tools you need to stand toe-to-toe with collection agencies. Properly used, the information in this book could save you thousands of dollars and earn you plenty of peace at home. I wish you luck.

Caveat

There are two kinds of bill collectors in this world: those who call directly from the place that gave you credit (department stores, banks, or whoever), and third-party collectors, those mercenaries who are hired by the original lenders when their in-house people give up. Most of the information you are about to read pertains only to the latter type, as they're the ones restricted by the Fair Debt Collections Practices Act (FDCPA). Original lenders and attorneys are not affected by this law. I heartily recommend that you take care of any accounts while they are still with the original lender. This will help preserve your credit to a certain extent.

When plotting evasion strategies, be sure to keep in mind which type of collector you're dealing with. If you're not sure, ask them whether they're calling from, for example, Penney's directly or from an agency that Penney's has hired to represent them.

Also, any evasion strategies that rely on the FDCPA to work cannot be used with business debts, as this particular federal law covers personal, not business, debt.

1

I Make Good Money, Why Am I Still In Debt?

Some people (most likely my relatives) wonder why I wrote a book about skipping out on debt. I mean, that's not really the American way, is it? Men (and women) are supposed to pay what they owe, do the honorable thing, and live up to their good names. Unfortunately, the American Protestant work ethic doesn't always make you successful. Sometimes it makes you a wage slave.

Most people I know are generally honest, expecting to be able to take people at their word and close a deal with a handshake. While that approach may work well in everyday life, it's a failure when it comes to personal finance and contract law.

On the back of nearly every credit card application and with each bank loan application, you will find columns of legal drivel, arcane incantations written in the tiniest print known to man, and sensible only to those who've gone to school for law or business finance. Do you really think that they expect the average American to fully understand the contract they're about to sign? Not for a moment. My guess is that they hope *nobody* can understand it. In that way, they can squeeze the most money out of the consumer, all the time claiming that "It's right there, in black and white." Who's doing the honorable thing here: the hardworking consumer who's trying to pay back his loan, or the lender's legal department, who're trying to chisel out an extra percent of interest?

While reading this book, I hope you pay some attention to why you're in this situation in the first place, if only so you can avoid this problem in the future. If we were discussing this over a cup of coffee, you might blame your situation on a dozen reasons: divorce, a bad harvest, being laid-off from your job, and so on. While these reasons may be partially responsible for your current financial problems, I'd suggest that you lay some of the blame at the door of your lender. That's right, your lender.

You can't blame your lender for loaning you money—that is, after all, what you asked them to do. However, once they provide you with a loan or a line of credit, most lenders slap on the leeches and try to bleed you in every way they can.

Three-quarters of credit card holders in America carry balances on their credit cards, balances which usually earn 18 percent interest. Strangely enough, if you deposit money at the bank that issued the card, they'll be happy to pay you 3 percent in a savings account or perhaps 5 percent in a CD. That's quite an income for a group of people who just sit around and make marks on paper all day. Imagine how much they'd make if they actually *worked* for a living. But I digress.

If you carry, say, an average balance of $1,000 on your credit card, then your bank is charging you $15 per month just for interest. Considering that your minimum payment on a balance that size is probably $20 or $30, it'll take you a helluva long time to get that balance down to zero.

Some cards charge annual fees. American Express, for example, costs $50 per year just to carry the card around in order to impress the relatives. Even if you never use it, that's $50 down the toilet.

But wait, there's more! If you're like me, you'll probably make two or three late payments per year. That's another $20 to $45 you may as well have thrown in the street.

How about other services? Has Citibank ever called you and offered to sell you travel services or, worse, some form of credit protection scam where you won't be held responsible for any new charges on your lost or stolen credit cards? I say it's a scam because federal law limits your liability in such a case to $50 per card, provided you notify the card issuers within 48 hours of the loss. Typically this "service" costs you $50 to $100 per year, and although it covers all cards in your wallet, you'd probably be better off just taking the lump. The last time *I* lost my wallet (or had it stolen) was 1987, and there wasn't a damn thing in it besides some business cards and an instant cash card.

When's the last time you bought something on a credit card? Did you know that you paid 3 to 4 percent more than you had to? Credit card issuers charge a fee to merchants in order to let them accept the cards as payment for purchases. The retailers, of course, pass the extra cost along to you in the form of higher prices. Four percent may not seem like much, but remember that $300 stereo you bought? That's like a $12 user fee sent directly to your credit card company. Next time you're in a ma and pa store, not one of the big chain stores, ask for a cash discount if you plan to pay by cash or check. You might just get one.

I think you're starting to get the idea. In the course of a year, you could end up paying $300 *or more* for useless services and usurious interest *on each card you have.* I don't know about you, but $300 is more than I make in a week, after taxes.

Watch that fine print, my friend, each and every time you borrow money. There's no such thing as a friendly bank. They're in business to make money, period, not to provide you with a sense of security. If you have some sort of financial emergency, your credit will be shut off and they'll use their hired goons to sue you and garnish your paycheck.

My friend Michael is a draftsman. He's got a pretty good job and has had it for five or six years. Recently, his wife left him and their two kids, taking off with a trucker after no more than an hour's notice. Michael was making payments on two new vehicles at the time, plus trailer payments, plus trying to keep his kids fed and clothed. Now he had to play "Mr. Mom" as well as hold down his full-time job. He fell behind on his car payments . . . and the bank repossessed both of them and sold them at auction, getting for both vehicles the equivalent of wholesale value on one of them. Total. Now he's stuck with a bill the size of a new car, but with no car to show for it. He probably won't be seeing a full paycheck for years.

Everybody has trouble once in awhile, but those who are deep in debt could find themselves losing everything. My advice to you is to get out of debt as quickly and painlessly as you can, then start saving money for emergency situations. Should you have some credit? Sure. But keep your credit cards clean and reserve them for emergencies *only*. That way they'll be there when you need them.

Inside a Collection Agency

On the extreme western edge of Minneapolis lurks a tower of corruption and severity, a sanctum of evil which, like a cancer cell, twists and sickens the lives of all it touches.

Well, maybe it's not quite that bad. How about a normal office building that houses a collection of stressed-out, sweaty people who do their best to share the misery they feel? That's probably closer to the truth.

Aggressive Agencies, Inc., takes up the whole eighth floor of one of the buildings in a nondescript office park in Minneapolis. In the same building are a theater, a steak house, and numerous other offices where the only real things produced are reams of paperwork. The buildings themselves are "Soviet Utopian"—hulking rectangles of concrete and glass that display all the life and imagination of a mannequin's torso.

To get to the offices of Aggressive Agencies, one must walk through a ritzy, marble-floored building lobby (complete with ice-queen receptionist and meaningless abstract sculpture) and take one of the four rickety elevators up to level eight. If the office park organization is rich enough to pony up thousands of dollars for bad sculpture, I don't know why they can't afford to grease the elevator pulleys. We used to ride the things about six times a day, including smoke breaks, and they continually rattled and groaned like a fat suburbanite's colon. Every day I waited for the *sproing!* of a cable snapping and the sickening plunge of an eight-story fall. Everybody who rode in them made little jokes as the cars screeched and rocked back and forth, but they were the kind of jokes you'd hear while waiting to be crucified.

Assuming you live long enough to arrive at the eighth floor, you're faced with two sets of double doors—one set wide open, one set closed. If you're applying for a job, paying a bill in person, trying to sell office products, or work in support services, you want the open doors. If you work on the collection "floor" or are carrying a big gun and a grudge against the people who made your life a living hell, you should choose the closed doors. They're not locked.

The collection floor is where all of the interesting stuff goes on. A hundred or more collectors are packed into cubicles under signs that read "Bad Checks," "Bank Cards," "Student Loans," and so on. Attached to the cubicles are little signs stating the collector's alias.

Almost no collectors work under their own names. During training, they ask you to pick an alias (which will be registered with the state) to use when you call people. This is supposed to ensure that collectors don't get threatening calls in the middle of the night . . . but there's a side-effect that also comes into play.

Working under a different name allows collectors to take on a different persona when they work. It's a pretty well-known fact of psychology that people will do things under a different name (or in a uniform) that they wouldn't do under their own. It somehow allows them to disassociate themselves from their acts.

Supervisors get actual desks in a corner of the room, veneered pressboard from OfficeMax or some such place. The area manager gets a slightly bigger desk on a raised dias. The psychological implications are almost insultingly obvious; he's the alpha male, the Chief, the Terminator. Of course, he fawns over clients and grovels before the owner of the agency, but never while any of his underlings can see him.

If a collector's not doing well enough (i.e., not hitting his "goal" often enough), the Chief tells the poor bastard's supervisor to make him disappear. They don't put a bullet through his head and sink him in a bog or anything, at least I don't think they do, but the guy in the cubicle next door, who was just this morning harassing Chinese debtors with statements like, "You speekee English, Chinee?" just never comes back from lunch. They fire a couple of people a week this way. After a few weeks of seeing your co-workers drop off the face of the earth, you get kinda nervous when the Chief comes around.

A collector's "goal" is a certain dollar amount that he needs to collect. At the end of each month, every collector cranks into high gear to do his best to "hit goal." Repeatedly failing to hit goal means he's going to disappear; hitting his goal means he starts getting commission on the amount he collects. As the end of the month approaches, collectors get desperate to get closer to their goal and thus are more willing to start cutting deals.

In the background you can hear the noises of people pretending to be hard at work—the clickety clack of keyboards, lots of muttering, and the occasional shout of "Just pay it, ma'am, just pay it!" The "floor" is filled with the bittersweet smell of warm computer gear, nervous sweat, and, near the bathrooms, human filth.

(Whichever high-buck architect designed the Aggressive offices must've been temporarily retarded when he drew in the bathrooms. There are probably a hundred men on the collection floor, many of them with middle-aged, clogged colons. They have access to one bathroom—three stalls and two urinals, all of which are in use constantly. The hot, moist air inside seems to be twice as dense as the air out on the floor. The smell is, well, it's indescribable.)

There may be a couple of trainees around, snuggled up next to a veteran collector, two to a cubicle, their faces showing shocked anxiety as they listen to the vet break federal law.

"I gotta slimy little debtor who thinks she's pretty clever," says the vet to the trainee, "but that bitch's in my

7

breakfast club. She's gettin' a call every morning, 9 A.M. I told her so, too."

When I was learning the trade, our trainer spent a day going over a piece of legislation called "The Fair Debt Collections Practices Act" (see Appendix A). This law, which was sponsored by a congressman who (we were told) didn't want to pay his creditors, makes it a federal offense to, among other things, threaten a citizen with repeated calls.

Never heard of it? I'm not surprised. For some reason it doesn't get mentioned in print, on television, or in day-to-day conversation, even though it can provide immense relief to the perhaps 25 million people in the United States who are getting hassled by bill collectors. Consumer Credit Counseling Services knows about it, and so do attorneys, but until you hire them, they won't say boo.

The veteran collector we were just talking about broke the law by threatening to make repeated calls. If a bill collector says to you, "I'm gonna call you every day until you pay this bill," you can sue the balls off of the agency he works for. Serious.

In any case, after the trainer carefully instructed us in just what we could and could not get away with legally, we got out to the floor and discovered it was all bullshit. Aggressive Agencies, at the time I worked there, was one of the most consistent lawbreakers in the city—they racked up stacks of "state complaints." My roommate at the time, Dan, who worked with another collection agency, couldn't believe the stuff we got away with on a daily basis. You see, we assumed that all debtors were ignorant about their rights under federal law. And almost without exception, they were.

From time to time, a collector strolls over to a different section than the one he's working in. He may be sharing information on a debtor with someone else, making plans for lunch, or arranging to pay his own overdue bills.

What? Collectors aren't the credit-conscious paragons of virtue that they portray themselves to be? Indeed they're not; many of the collectors with whom I worked were making payments of their own to their co-workers. Sometimes things got even worse.

One day a bunch of us were going to run down to the local Dairy Queen for lunch. "Kent Black," a chain-smoking dwarf who worked Citibank accounts, had a minivan, and so some of us caught rides with him. "Jason Hutchinson," who worked Penney's and Dayton's accounts with me, said he'd meet us there. We left him wandering around the parking ramp, looking for his car.

Jason was a lunatic—he worked two full-time jobs just to support his ugly-tempered wife and two rotten kids. It wasn't like he drove a Porsche or anything; his car was a mid-70s Buick. God knows where all of his money went, but the stress of working two jobs made him beat up debtors with a desperation known only to Adolf Hitler when the Allies were closing in on his bunker. He had a cleft palate (Jason, not Hitler), or maybe he was partially deaf, because when he started screaming over the phone, he was completely incomprehensible. Whatever poor sod he was dealing with just had to sit there and take it, because hanging up on him just made him worse. But I digress; we left him wandering around the ramp.

We got our chili dogs or whatever at Dairy Queen and joked about why Jason wasn't showing up. He couldn't find his car, or he locked the keys inside, or he had to stop off and pick up a few things for the wife. When our lunch hour was up, we returned to find him yelling at someone over the phone. It turned out that while he was harassing other people for money, the finance company that held the paper on his car had sent a tow truck to repossess it.

Jason got "disappeared" a few days later, so I never found out if he got his rusty behemoth back. It was probably just as well. After the repo, he was a broken man who walked around wearing an icy mask of normalcy. Occasionally, one of us would catch him weeping at his desk.

3

More Than You Need to Know About Your Credit

In one way or another, your credit got you into this mess. The bad check, the delinquent student loan, and the repossessed Chevy pickup were all possible because of credit.

Bill collectors do a lot of talking about your credit. They say it like the words are capitalized: "Your Credit."

"Until you take care of this matter, it may adversely affect Your Credit." Everybody's heard that line; at least I'm guessing *you* have, or you wouldn't need this book. But what the hell is your credit, exactly, and how is it affected by the stuff you do?

When somebody talks about "your credit," what they mean is your credit history, available (for a fee) from any of a handful of credit reporting agencies (often called credit bureaus) in the United States. If you've been turned down for credit recently, the agency that reported on you is required by law to send you a free copy of your history. Look on the rejection letter; the name and address of the reporting agency will be on it. Send them a certified letter, explaining that you have been recently turned down for credit. Give them your name, Social Security number, and address, and be sure to enclose a photocopy of the rejection letter. You should receive your report in a couple of weeks. Here's a sample copy of a real credit report (the name, Social Security number, and address have been redacted):

* 323 EQUIFAX CREDIT INFORMATION SERVICES,   PO BOX 740241,
  5505 PEACHTREE DUNWOODY RD STE 600,ATLANTA,GA,30374-0241,800-685-1111

SINCE 02/16/89 FAD 12 02/96   FN-328
CRT RPTD 12/95
DAT RPTD 11/95

TELEPHONE NUMBER
BDS-01/00/69,SSS   SSN VER - Y
01 ES-

*SUM-02/87-11/96,PR/OI-NO,COLL-NO,FB-NO, ACCTS:10,HC$200-11765, 1-ZERO. 6-ONES.
 1-TWO, 2-NINES, HIST DEL- 2-THREES, 1-FOUR, 1-FIVE.
FIRM / IDENT CODE   CS RPTD LIMIT HICR BAL $ DLA MR (30-60-90+)MAX DEL
ECOA/ACCOUNT NUMBER   OPND P/DUE TERM   24 MONTH HISTORY

ATT UNIVSL*444ON358 R2 11/96 500 — 522 09/96 18 (01-01-00)
I/539882005471   04/95 15 15   ***32********/************
  CLOSED ACCOUNT

CAP 1 BANK*850BB24906 R1 10/96 — 223 0 04/96 24
I/5291071316914884   09/94 — —
  ACCOUNT CLOSED BY CONSUMER
  CREDIT CARD

TRACY STAT*620BB7769 R1 10/96 300 — 278 09/96 34
I/700000717061293   12/93 — 25
  LINE OF CREDIT

RNB-DAYTON*613DC15358 R9 07/93 — 200 0 04/91
I/76720144210   02/87 — —
  PAID CHARGE OFF
  CHARGED OFF ACCOUNT

DISCOVR CD*155BB3747 R1 03/93 1500 — 0 02/93 12   08/90-R3
U/601100733851   12/89 — —   ***2****2***/*3****432***
  CLOSED ACCOUNT

CITIBANK *906BB115 R1 03/91 500 — 0 03/91 21
I/412800258038   05/89 — —
  CLOSED ACCOUNT

TEXACO *905OC777 R9 03/91 — 225 0 02 91 (00-00-03)
I/53656194501289   12/89 — —   55*5********.************
  PAID CHARGE OFF

J C PENNEY*906DC185 R1 08/90 — 260 0 08/90 12
I/56-579082828820   02/87 — —   32**********.************

  REVOLVING TOTALS   2800 908 800
                        15   40

FRSTBK NA *616BB5379 I0 08/96 — 11765 11765
I/46898057499   09/93 0 —
  STUDENT LOAN - PAYMENT DEFERRED

NW BK SD *616BB651 I1 07/90 — 2018 0 04.90 01
I/40122970401   — 95

  INSTALLMENT TOTALS   — 11765 11765
                        —   —

  GRAND TOTALS   2800 12673 12565
                  15   40

*INQS-SPRINT LD 910UT10942 12/02/96   AMERICAN 190ON1661 02/21 96
 FIRST USA 458ON7296 12/13/95 ANB   458ON5282 11/18/95
 CITICORP 404ON168 12 29/94 J C PENNEY 291DC41 12/19/94
 &

Figure 1

"There are three different formats for this report (called a "bureau" by collectors and skiptracers), but all of them contain the same information: your name, address, previous addresses, Social Security number, place of employment (in this case, Frey's Best Honey), credit history, civil litigation history (if you've been sued or gone bankrupt, and when), and the names and dates of any requests for copies of your file within the last couple of years. In order to request a copy of your report, a lender or collection agency needs to provide at least two of the following: your street address, name, and Social Security number. If two or more factors match a report on file at that agency, they send out the report.

The credit history section of your bureau is a list of companies that have extended credit to you. Each entry lists (in addition to the company name) a partial account number, your credit limit, the status of that account (listed as "paid charge off," "open account," "settled account," "closed by consumer," and other terms), the balance owed, and a two-letter combination indicating how late you've ever made a payment.

The two-letter code usually starts with an "R" (less frequently it starts with an "I"), so if on a particular account you made one payment a month late, the code will probably say "R2" (creditspeak for "It took 'em two months to send a payment"). If an account is in "in-house" collections, the code will probably be "R5." If your account goes to a third-party agency, it'll be changed to "R9." These codes are to be avoided, if possible—if you have one R9 on your bureau, you *might* still be able to get a new line of credit. If you have two or more, your credit is pretty much shot. It's for that reason that I recommend you pay your account off when it's still in-house (if you plan to pay it at all). Sometimes this just isn't possible, though, and you have to take your lumps.

Bill collectors let you think that when you pay a bill at their agency, your credit will be cleared up. This is not the case, however—not by a long shot. When you pay an account, its status will be changed from "profit-and-loss writeoff" or "charge-off" to "paid charge-off," but the two-letter code will still be an R9. Not a significant improvement—even if you pay off every account you have in collections, those R9s will still be there, and credit will be tougher to get than pork chops in a synagogue, at least until stuff starts dropping off your bureau in accordance with the seven-year limit.

According to federal law, all information contained in your bureau has a shelf life of seven years. This is seven years from the date of last activity, not from the time you opened the account. If someone's hassling you about a loan you haven't made a payment on in six and a half years, ignore them. In six more months, all records will be removed (assuming the reporting agency remembers to do so). It'll be just like it never happened.

On the other hand, maybe you don't really need to sit around and wait at all. Rule *numero uno* in the credit area is: "If it ain't written down, it never happened." Not all companies subscribe to a reporting agency. It costs them administrative time and money each time they update your account, and some companies just figure it's not worth the hassle. AT&T, Sprint, and MCI don't report on long-distance accounts (as of this writing), for example, and neither do most utility companies. Neither does Amoco, most collection agencies, or rent-to-own stores. Many small-town banks do not. No mail-order book, coin, stamp, or CD companies do. Sure, having an outstanding balance at any of these places will hinder you from getting credit *at that company*, but who cares? If it's not recorded on your bureau, it never happened, as far as anyone else knows.

There are always people standing in line to give you credit. If you're not sure whether a lender reports to a credit bureau, call 'em up and ask. Make up some goofy story about how you want to make sure that your good payment history is preserved . . .

The Credit Game: Cheating

It is possible to open up a completely new credit file for yourself. All you need to do is change two out of the three variables that lenders put down on the request form. Bear in mind that any actions you make in this direction qualify as fraud, a criminal offense, though no one ever seems to get prosecuted for it—the companies concerned generally don't feel it's worth their time and court costs. When I was a collector, I used to find a couple of bureaus a week that had multiple Social Security numbers. Obviously someone didn't know that they needed to change two variables instead of just one. But none of our clients were ever very interested in criminal prosecution; they just wanted their money back.

I recommend changing your address and Social Security number, as using credit cards with someone else's name on them can be inconvenient at times. Go down to Mailboxes Etc. or a similar mail-drop company and rent a drawer; they'll issue you what looks like a street address and apartment number.

Most credit lenders want to see working phone numbers, both for one's residence and business. You can either put yours down or get an account with an answering service for maybe twenty bucks a month—they don't care who they answer for but will simply pick up when your line rings and say "Deadbeat International" (or whatever your company name is) in a professional manner, talk to the caller, and take a message. Just like a real business.

Next, change your Social Security number. The first five numbers of your SS# are not random but coded; the first three numbers indicate in which state you applied for your number, and the next two represent the year. The safest method, then, is to modify the last four numbers, which don't mean anything.

Cool! Now when you apply for credit, the request will come back "No Report" or something similar. In many ways, having no credit is better than having bad credit. Start off by applying for department store and gas cards, which are the easiest to get. After making small charges and timely payments for six months or so, you should be able to start getting bank cards (Visa, Mastercard, and Discover). Presto! You're a valued member of society again.

There is another way to regain credit. You've probably

seen ads for people who promise to clean up or fix your credit. If you inquire further, it turns out they want $500 and six months or a year to do it. Here's how to do what they do:

Get a copy of your credit report and write down the negative items. Write a letter to the reporting agency stating that you have found some errors on your report, then list the negative items and reasons why the entries are incorrect (in most cases they're probably correct, so you'll have to lie). Typical excuses are: "Don't remember opening this account," "No knowledge of account," and "Had this account, but never made a late payment." As in all communications with credit reporting agencies, make photocopies of all correspondence and send everything certified mail. Verifying your credit history is something that costs them time and money, so if they have a chance to weasel out of the job, they will.

This maneuver is available thanks to The Fair Credit Reporting Act (FCRA), federal legislation that was enacted because credit bureaus were such rotten record keepers that they were screwing up people's credit via bookkeeping errors. The FCRA states that credit reporting agencies must investigate any credit entry that a consumer indicates is inaccurate. They are allowed to discard any "spurious" claims, though, so try to stay within the realm of possibility—no CIA conspiracies or space aliens kidnapping your account number.

When they receive your letter, the agency will have to contact representatives of each company listed in your letter in order to verify the information in your file. If the original lender never responds or doesn't respond within a "reasonable amount of time" (generally 30 days), then that entry drops off your credit history. If they do verify the information, it stays on your report. The agency will notify you of any changes made in this way, and will provide a copy of your "new" credit report.

Now go through the whole process again, and keep doing it until all negative references are taken off your bureau. The original lender may swear up and down that the information is correct, and it may well be, but sooner or later they're going to get tired of verifying it and it will have to be removed. Your odds of a late or nonexistent verification are better if you send your letter to the reporting agency in late June or late November. By the time the original lender has to deal with the paperwork, huge numbers of people are going to be out of the office on summer or Christmas vacation. With luck, the verification requests will just get lost in the shuffle.

Now is probably as good a time as any to introduce the subject of "supplementing one's income via theft." Strange as it may seem, while both shoplifting and robbery are criminal offenses, ordering stuff without paying for it is not. You could, for example, rack up hundreds of dollars worth of phone bills as well as amass a fine collection of books, stamps, coins, and CDs for no more than the cost of postage, and it would never affect your credit. You might get sued, obviously, but if your bill at any one company is less than $100, the chances of that occurring are virtually nil. If you use variations on your name (M. or Maxwell instead of Max, for example) and street address or "accidentally" misspell your own last name, you can often reap two or three harvests from the same company.

Credit is a game, nothing more, and if you keep your wits about you, it's not that tough to win.

4

How'd They Find Me?

It's a familiar story: in order to escape the bill collectors, you quit your job, change your name, and move from Baltimore to Duluth. Three days later, the little old lady from across the street arrives to welcome you to the neighborhood. Along with a fruitcake in the shape of a pig, she brings a message to call so-and-so from Penney's. That afternoon, you start getting calls at work about your Chase Visa account.

"What the hell?" you think. "How in God's name did they track me halfway across the country?"

It's easier than you think. When a debtor tries running out on his debts, or the agency doesn't have a valid phone number for him, a little skiptracing is in order. But dodging out on collectors is a lot easier when you know what they're looking for. In order to beat The Man, you've got to be The Man.

Skiptracing involves a number of steps. The higher the account balance, the more steps are justified in the process. At Aggressive Agencies, only the first two or three steps would be performed for a balance of less than a hundred dollars; anything more than that meant we could go all the way. The following (imaginary) example shows how I'd "skip down" a debtor.

Leonard Hauptmann owes $1,250 on his Citibank Visa. The last known number for him has been discon-

19

nected, but mail sent to him in Davenport, Iowa, has not been returned, nor has the post office notified the agency of his forwarding address. This indicates that either a) he's at the same address but has either no phone or a different number, b) he moved, but didn't forward his mail and the new tenants are throwing it away, or c) the U.S. Postal Service is staffed by idiots who are sending his mail to Tibet. His phone number may as well be the only point of contact; we'll send him letters, but even if the address is good, he's probably not going to send any money unless someone calls him up.

The first three numbers of his Social Security number tell me that he applied for his card in Montana. I may have to look for him there, as debtors will often run closer to home when they get into trouble, but I'll try the Davenport area first.

Step 1: Call Directory Assistance in the city where the debtor last received mail. When most folks move, they stay in the area. If the debtor isn't listed and the city is small and rural, get the numbers for people with the same last name—there's a good chance they're related. If not, get the numbers for the public library and property tax assessor's office.

Lennie's last known address was in Davenport, Iowa, a city just big enough that calling someone with the same last name probably won't do any good—the operator says she's got 15 or 20 Hauptmanns listed. I get the phone numbers for the library and the tax assessor's office.

Step 2: Call the library. Strangely enough, libraries hire people to sit around in the reference section and answer questions for people, especially bill collectors. It seems kind of sick that sweet old Mrs. Monahan from Saturday Story Hour would be ratting on you, but life is hard, pal.

When the librarian gets on the phone, I tell her that I

want to "criss-cross" an address. She asks me the address, and I give him Hauptmann's. She confirms the bad number we have listed, which is no real surprise. Rather than an official U.S. West Criss Cross directory, it turns out that the librarian's working out of a Polk Directory, so it lists all the people who live at that address and where Hauptmann and his wife work. Good deal.

Step 3: Call Directory Assistance again, looking for the numbers for both places of employment and/or any listings under his wife's name, which is not Hauptmann, but Fergel.

DA tells me that there's a Fergel listed at that address, but that it's nonpublished. I get both work numbers before hanging up.

Step 4: Call both places of employment. According to federal law, I can talk to either him or his wife about his little problem with Citibank, so if either of them are still employed where the Polk Directory said they were, the bill's as good as paid. Nobody likes to get calls like this at work, especially when I insult their co-workers and boss.

I call up both places, but neither Hauptmann nor Fergel is employed with them any longer. Using my rural background to its best advantage, I get real folksy and start to jaw with the secretary in Hauptmann's office. Turns out he's still in town; she thinks he's doing construction work and hasn't heard that he's moved. I thank her politely and hang up. I've still got a big goose egg as far as information goes.

Step 5: Call the property tax assessor's office and find out who owns the property at Lenny's address. Some cities won't give this information over the phone, but most will.
The clerk tells me that the property is owned by a

Reginald Maltin and that his tax bills are sent to a Davenport address. That'd be Lenny's landlord. It's quite possible that he has Hauptmann's phone number, but will he give it to me?

Step 6: Back to Directory Assistance, this time for a listing for Reginald Maltin.

Turns out he's unlisted. If Lenny didn't owe so much money, that'd be the end of my search—we'd just have to send him a bunch of letters. His high balance, though, allows me to request a copy of his bureau.

Step 7: Request a bureau on Hauptmann, listen to area manager scream about having to pay two bucks for it, and wait a couple of days.

Hauptmann's bureau is full of bad debt, so it looks like no one else is having any better luck finding him than I am. About the only thing he's got that he's still making payments on is a car loan at the Landshark Finance Company. Finance companies are usually pretty good about sharing information.

Step 8: Call the finance company's "skip line," tell them where I'm calling from, and pray.

The skiptracer on the other end of the phone proves to be helpful enough; turns out he's got the Hauptmanns' new number. I thank him and hang up, intending to give ol' Lenny a big surprise.

So that's what you're up against. In addition to the previous-mentioned sources, people can get information about you from the local cops, the post office, the college you attend or attended, your next-door neighbor, your answering service, your kids, the Department of Motor Vehicles, and Uncle

Sam's locator service for military personnel. Think of it as Everyone vs. You. Assume that everyone you know and every company or government office you've come in contact with will rat on you if given half a chance. Paranoia is the key to successful evasion.

How to Not Be Found

Honest, Godfearing people leave a paper trail a mile wide; most crooked ones do too, as they don't know enough about The System to avoid leaving traces. Even clever, paranoid people leave clues to their whereabouts, though they're tougher to find. Never assume you're invisible.

There's no way that you can prevent anyone from finding you; not even the Federal Witness Protection Program can do that. Anyone can be found if the person looking for them wants them bad enough. The nice thing, at least as far as debt-dodging is concerned, is that bill collectors generally don't care whether they find you or not. They want to spend their time focusing on people who sound like they're going to pay, not on tracking some poor schmuck halfway across the country. If they find him and he can't or won't pay them, they've just wasted their time and the agency's money.

It is possible, usually, to hide yourself from someone who's not looking for you very hard. The following are some suggestions:

- Get an unlisted phone number, and be careful who you give it to. Contrary to popular belief, nobody, but nobody, can get your or anyone's unlisted number from the phone company. Train your relatives not to give it out to people claiming to be your buddies—the chances are good that they're bill collectors. Have ma and pa take a message if it's so important.

  Remember that if you give your nonpub number to other creditors, the chances are good that they'll give it to whoever is looking for you, so give them a fake one.

They'll never use it unless they need to contact you, which usually only happens when you're late on a payment to them (in which case you don't want to hear from them).

- If, for some strange reason, you can't restrict access to your phone number, screen your calls through an answering machine. Your message should say something like, "You have reached 555-2734, please leave a message." By no means should you leave your name on the message. You see, collectors are not only restricted as to the amount of information they can leave on a machine at a number they're not sure is good, but they're not likely to call any more frequently than they have to (every two weeks or so). Remember, they want to concentrate their effort on people who will pay, not numbers with anonymous messages. Unless they're sure you live there, they're not likely to waste much time leaving entertaining messages. Even if they do know you live there, they can't get any more information if they can't talk to you.

- Live in a big city. Once a collector starts making skiptracing calls around Mayberry, he's sure to stumble across people who'll tell him more than he wants to know about you and your place of employment. One time I called a small-town library to do some skiptracing and the guy I was looking for happened to be checking out a book there. The librarian was more than happy to fetch him to the phone, and he got mad as hell. The anonymity of even a mid-sized city is the debtor's friend.

- Deny everything. When a collector gets a listing from directory assistance, he knows that the person he's calling is quite possibly the wrong guy. He really can't do anything until you admit owing the money or he can prove that you're the "Bill Smith" that he's after. If he goes ahead with collection procedures and you're the wrong guy (even if you're Bill Smith Jr. and he's looking for your dad), he can get slapped with a big state complaint and a fat lawsuit.

That being the case, you may wish to simply deny any knowledge of the debt or of any personal information the collector might have. Tell him he's got the wrong guy. He'll ask you to give him your Social Security number. Refuse to do so by telling him that he's just a ripoff artist who will use it to commit crimes. He then will probably give you what he's got down for your Social Security number. Tell him it's absolutely wrong.

About the same time as you get the first call from the agency, you'll get a "notification of intent to pursue collection activity" letter in the mail. It will say that you've got 30 days to deny or dispute the debt. By all means do so. When the notification letter arrives, send back a certified letter disavowing any knowledge of the debt. This in itself may be enough to get collection activities dropped, but at the very least it will postpone collection activity until they get a copy of the original credit application.

Remember, this approach will only work if a collector has had to skip you down (without getting a copy of your bureau). Don't try it if you've been getting calls from the original creditor. If he eventually can prove that you're the guy he's looking for, he'll probably be mad as hell. You may wish to be sure that you'll be able to pay the bill at that time, as he'll probably make your life miserable until you do. Or, better yet, "cease" him (see Chapter 5).

- Hide behind a P.O. box or mail drop address. While the post office will, for a fee, give out your real address (at least the real address you put down on the form) to anyone who requests it, they won't do it over the phone. Most collection agencies won't allow their skiptracers to go to the trouble of sending a letter with money enclosed, so they'll run up against a blank wall. Companies that operate a mail-drop service, as far as I know, will not release information about the people who rent an address there.

- Refuse to give information about yourself to people who call or show up on your doorstep. Remember the friendly folks who put out the Polk Directory? No sense having the whole world know where you live and work.

- Notify the county courthouse (and, if you're a student, your college's registrar's office) that you want to restrict the amount of information that they can release to the public. I found numerous debtors through the registrar's office of their local college. In one instance, the clerk didn't want to give me the information that I "knew" was public, so I insinuated that I had had a sexual relationship with the male student I was looking for a couple of years before. I told her that I had the results to some medical tests that he'd probably better know about. I got his number.

  The amount of information that can be released to the public varies from state to state, but there's usually a form you can fill out that will cut your losses to an absolute minimum. On the other hand, while it's probably a crime to lie to the Department of Motor Vehicles about your address, you could certainly leave bad information with the registrar's office. It's been my experience that college registrar offices send a lot of mail, but they never call, so make sure they get a good P.O. box number for you.

- Train your kids not to give information over the phone. I always loved to have a kid answer the phone when I was calling a debtor. I'd talk real sweet to them, just like I was a buddy of their daddy's, and they'd generally tell me where he worked and what his phone number was (thus saving my penny-pinching manager a quarter for the directory assistance charge). I'd call up the work number, yell at whoever answered, and generally try to raise as much hell between him and his co-workers as I could. When he came to the phone, I'd beat him up a little and tell him that we now had the option to sue him and garnish his wages. I have to laugh, today, thinking about how surprised some of them sounded when they found out who was on the phone.

If a bill collector finds out where you work, you're through, pal. You may as well just pay him whatever he wants, because your life's going to be a living hell until he goes away. If your nonpub number somehow winds up in the hands of a collector, you can change it the next day. But if he gets ahold of your work number, you're meat.

- When calling a collection agency, use a pay phone. Many agencies now use Caller ID or a similar call-tracing service provided by the friendly phone company. In most areas, dialing *69 will also give the number of the last caller. I could go into a long song and dance about how you can get a service (for a monthly fee) from the phone company that blocks Caller ID, or how you can punch in a code before you call someone so they can't use the *69 trick, but the monthly service is a ripoff, and it's probably safer just to use a pay phone and bill the call to your home number.

- If you make any payments on a bill, send a money order, not a check. There are two reasons for this: first, your check probably lists your correct mailing address and phone number, and second, if for some reason you can't make any further payments, the agency now knows where you bank and what your account number is. If you get sued, they can send the sheriff down to your bank with a writ to take the amount of the judgment right out of your checking account. If that happens, you'll probably bounce checks all over town, each costing $15 to $20 for a NSF (nonsufficient funds) service charge. Sending a check to a collection agency is like giving an extortionist the combination to your wall safe.

- If you're in the armed services, don't give any indication of that on your initial application for credit. That means don't put them down as an employer, and give your parents' address and phone number rather than an APO or FPO box number. As you know, when you signed up you had to sign a paper that, in essence, stated that you were not joining the military to skip out on any debts. If your commanding officer gets a call from a collection agency, you'll *wish* you were just a civilian getting calls at work.

We had one collector named "Charles Woods" who'd work everybody's army accounts. He'd been in the military, so he knew the lingo and the system of organization. In one case I remember, he got ahold of some debtor's sergeant. Sarge called the debtor into his office, made him write a series of post-dated checks for the full amount of the debt, and then stated that he, Sarge, would mail the checks each month. If one of them bounced, the guy was looking at time in the stockade.

- When you move, notify each person or company individually rather than filling out the change-of-address card. You really should be doing this anyway, as the Post Office has a way of screwing things up. In any case, taking this step ensures that if an agency sends you an envelope that says "Address Correction Requested" or some similar thing on the front, the Post Office will be unable to notify them of your new address, because they've received no official notice telling them where you're going.

I have never known of an account where a collection agency sued a debtor whose phone number and place of employment were unknown. The advantage to not being found lies in the fact that they don't know if you're being contacted at all until you respond. For all they know, the collection letters they send every couple of weeks are just piling up on top of some stranger's fridge. If you just lie low, the chances are very good that they will send you six or eight letters, then walk away in frustration. This philosophy has the added bonus of causing them to waste a couple of dollars on postage.

All in all, there is no one foolproof way to never be skiptraced. The above suggestions will all help, but anyone with enough time, resources, and motivation can defeat them. Luckily, bill collectors usually don't have enough time, resources, or motivation. Skiptracing is generally a money loser for them, so after running into a few dead ends, they're liable to give up.

5 Bill Collector Psychology

In order to win a duel with a collector, you've got to know his attitudes and beliefs as well as the tools he can use against you. The reason most people lose the collection game, even if they want to pay their debt, is because they're less fighting a duel than getting ambushed.

There you are, trying to make the best of a bad situation, trying to put food on the table and new tires on the Chevy, and all of a sudden you, your spouse, and your boss are getting abused by a phone jockey who talks like Jack Webb.

He's tough, he's got an answer for every excuse you give, and he wields guilt and sarcasm like icepicks. *He* always pays *his* bills; *he* wouldn't be able to sleep at night if *he* had problems like yours. It must be nice to have a life so uncomplicated by debt (or a soul, for that matter).

Well, as we've already seen, bill collectors don't pay their bills any more frequently than the rest of us. Those who do pay their bills pay with money made by lies, manipulation, and sadism.

At all third party collection agencies of which I'm aware, collectors have a chance to earn commission on what they bring in. Any collector who claims not to get some sort of commission is either lying or an idiot. My friend Dan, for example, made more money his first year collecting than his father did teaching high school that year after 17 years on the job. The income range for collectors who are any good is roughly $35-60K.

Collectors at many agencies also get bonuses for people who send money by overnight delivery or Western Union. At Aggressive Agencies, the person who got the most "fast cash" in this manner received $100. This was determined each month, so a collector who trained himself to demand money immediately could conceivably net an extra $1,200 per year.

So your collector, then (when and if he finally gets ahold of you), is likely to a) demand payment in full, and b) tell you it must be sent via some sort of overnight delivery.

Good collectors press for payment in full until it's made abundantly clear to them that some sort of payment plan is called for. You see, they truly believe that you can access the money within a short period of time. Collectors believe that "their" debtors are lazy and stupid (even those who are doctors and lawyers), and they treat them accordingly. Every collector knows what he can get away with, legally and illegally, and knows that 99 percent of his debtors don't have the slightest idea about the law.

Further, they believe that any failure on your part to pay a bill is due to stubbornness or forgetfulness, not poverty. They're sure that if they just make your life miserable for a couple of months, you'll just cut them a check. That being said, here are some typical motivational ploys and the ways to defeat them:

- Collectors want to put you on the defensive from the moment the call begins. Unless they control the conversation, they don't make any money. Much of their game plan is simply to sit back, let you make excuses, and respond to each one in turn. When they've worn you out, then they start trying to see what kind of payments you're capable of.

  At Aggressive we were taught to make a "psychological pause" after introducing ourselves and stating the reason we were calling. This pause was nothing more than waiting, silently, for the debtor to start offering excuses or intentions to pay. Our trainer knew that silence in the course of a conversation is uncomfortable to most people, and that generally the debtor would try to do something to break it. Nine times out of ten, the ploy worked.

Your best defense is to say nothing. Force the collector to break the silence. You see, collectors play a largely *reactive* game. They've got a pat answer for every statement you give, but if you give them nothing to respond to, it flusters them and makes them more prone to making a (possibly illegal) mistake. Silence is your friend.

- "I need you to send this money FedEx/Western Union/etc. because . . ." Pure bullshit. He's in it for the money. Unless you're talking to the agency's *attorney*, there's no reason to send money other than by first class mail. It's a total scam and a waste of your money to do otherwise; I can't express it any clearer than that.

- Statements like, "Failure to respond to this matter *may* further damage your credit," "*How would you like it if* we sent the sheriff down to your job with a summons of complaint," and "Are you *currently* having your wages garnished" all use what are called "qualifier words" (which are in italics). Careful examination of these phrases will show you that, while they certainly sound scary, they don't really mean anything. You see, the FDCPA states that collectors cannot make threats that they don't intend to carry out. Since the collector doesn't decide who gets sued or how one's credit is affected by any particular action, he can't make any threats. All he can do is make statements that *sound* like threats but which really hold no meaning. Anytime a collector uses qualifier words like "may," "can," "might," and even "I'm going to recommend," you can feel free to mentally delete the entire sentence. He can recommend that you be taken into the woods and shot, but no one's going to take him seriously. Only the attorney makes those decisions.

They are hoping that you concentrate on the emotionally laden parts of the sentence like "legal action," "wage garnishment, or "deadbeat" rather than on what they're actually saying. If you realize that by inserting these qualifier words into their statements they are effectively negating the meaning of that statement, then there's no reason to get worried or upset by whatever words happen to also be in the sentence.

One thing to watch out for, though, is talking to the agency's attorney. You can play games for months with the collectors—they're just hired stooges. Don't play games with the attorney. You'll get maybe one chance to talk to him before they sue (if they weren't going to sue, you'd have never heard his name to begin with). He won't be using qualifier words either. He'll probably say, "We are going to sue you." According to federal law, collectors cannot claim to be attorneys. If you're not sure whether the person you're speaking to is an attorney or not, ask.

I have known some collectors who would claim to be attorneys, but most wouldn't dare. In any case, if you're talking with someone who says he's an attorney and says that they're definitely going to sue you, you'd better make a deal.

- "I can't give you a payment plan because . . ." Every collector is authorized to set up or accept virtually any kind of payment plan. The reason they don't like to do so is that they'd rather just get the money and never hear from you again. People who are on payment plans miss payments, make late payments, go bankrupt, and just plain disappear. To the collector, that means more work for the same return.

   Before putting anyone on a payment plan, most collectors want a whole bunch of information, sometimes even how much you spend on your water bill each month. They're trying to see what you can *afford* to pay rather than what you *offered* to pay. They'll always want to know your place of employment, whether you work full-time, how much you make per hour, and your phone number at work. This information tells them whether you're a candidate for a wage garnishment action should you fail to make your payments. They may call and verify the information you give them, too, so if you choose to lie, you should tell lies that will stand up to a cursory check.

In order to have your wages garnished, all of the following criteria needs to apply to you: 1) you are not self-employed (who's going to fill out his own garnishment papers?), 2) you are employed full-time, 3) you make over minimum wage, and 4) they know *where* you work. If at all possible, I recommend not letting them verify #4.

Even if you only work part-time or make minimum wage, it's unwise to let a collector know where you work. Think about it: you *have* to go to work, and when at work, you *have* to answer the phone. If you don't answer the phone at work, your boss or co-worker will, and the collector will beat *them* up. That's not going to help you have a good time at the office Christmas party.

I recommend that you pretend to be self-employed. Say you do pet grooming in your home or something like that. Feel free to elaborate that you're on welfare or Social Security. People on the government dole are virtually payment-free; no one bothers to beat them up because they don't have any money.

• Don't say something like, "If I send you five bucks a month, you *have* to take it. You can't sue me if I'm making payments." They sure as hell *can* sue you if you're making payments. No collector likes to get people set up on $5 or $10 payment schedules because they may drag on for years. Like I said before, debtors on payment plans are high-maintenance. The collector doesn't want to have to call you every month to remind you to send in your five bucks. It's a waste of his time, and he'll resent it.

Always remember that a battle with a bill collector is a battle of wits, and they're expecting you to show up unarmed. They expect that you will know nothing about the FDCPA (see Appendix A), that you will be honest and forthright in your dealings with them, and that you can be manipulated rather easily. It's not too difficult to prove them wrong. Just remember that it's like talking to the cops: everything you say can *and will* be used against you. Everything you say *will* be documented for review at a future time. If you have any lying to do, make sure you remember what it is you said so they can't trap you at some future time.

6 Beating the Bill Collector

Now that you've got some background information, we'll look at your best strategies for minimizing your payment or evading the debt altogether. The feds have given you some pretty big guns with which to fight back, and I heartily recommend that you do so.

The following strategies should be looked at as a "quick fix" only. Just because you stop someone from harassing you doesn't mean the bill goes away. In some cases it does, if the original creditor or the agency doesn't report to the credit bureau, but overall I've found that bills are like zombies: when you least expect it, they'll claw their way out of the grave and come calling. After a long enough time, every corpse rests in peace, but whether you have the endurance to wait that long is another question.

- When I was a kid, I always opened my biggest Christmas presents first. Along the same lines, I'm giving you the biggest gift right away: ceases.

   According to the FDCPA, you can prevent a bill collector from ever calling you again about a particular bill by just telling him to get lost. This is what's known as a "cease." You can't just say it in the vernacular, though, as collectors hate ceases and will try to weasel out of them if they think that they can make a good case for your not really meaning to cease them. You should say something like this:

> "Under the auspices of the Fair Debt Collections Practices Act, I hereby cease you from further contact."

That's it. Then hang up, write the same statement down on paper, and send it to the collector by certified mail. As you might expect, some collectors will pretend that they never heard the cease (i.e., they'll purposely not document it in your file) and will continue to come after you. If you have the ability to record phone conversations, I recommend that you record yourself ceasing the collector. That way, if you keep getting calls (until your certified cease shows up in the mail), you can get the agency's manager on the phone, play the tape, and threaten to sue his balls off.

When the certified cease arrives, the agency knows they've got to put up or shut up. Either they sue you or they send your file back to Penney's labeled as "ceased contact." They're not allowed to contact you in any way unless they'll be suing, and in that case you'll speak with the agency attorney. They can't send you letters, they can't do any further skiptracing, and they certainly can't call.

This is not a strategy you want to use if it's likely that you'll be sued (see Chapter Four), but if they don't know anything about you or you're pretty much "sue-proof," it works just dandy. Also remember that while third-party collection agencies are bound by this law, original lenders like Penney's and Citibank are not. If you try to cease them, they'll just laugh at you. Make sure you know whether your collector is "in-house" or "third party" before using any of your options under the FDCPA.

- They got you. They know where you work, they're ready

to sue, and the attorney is giving you one last call before signing the papers. Is now the time to send them a check for the balance due? Heck no! Try to get a settlement.

When I was getting a lot of calls from collectors, knowing about settlements could've saved me about a thousand dollars. The theory behind a settlement is pretty simple: you pay one big chunk of money that accounts for something between 50 and 80 percent of what you owe, and you'll never be contacted about the rest of the money. It'll still show up on your credit report as being owed, but you'll never get any more calls or letters about it.

Remember that paying a bill that has gone to collections does not improve your credit significantly. Also remember that within seven years of the time you settle, the debt will disappear completely (maybe within three years if you make the credit reporting agency verify it with the company). Further, rest assured that any time you want to pay the rest of the balance, the company will be happy to take your money. If you win the lottery a couple years from now, go ahead and pay it.

There's only one thing that's not fantastic about a settlement, and that's the fact that if you want to take out some sort of bank loan in the future, the loan officer will often make you pay the outstanding balance on the account you settled. Still, you're no worse off than you would have been to pay the whole thing, and thanks to inflation you're actually coming out a little bit ahead.

It's likely that no one will offer a settlement to you until they've hit you for payment in full a few times. That doesn't mean you can't offer to make a settlement deal. Not all companies will accept settlements, but most will. Dayton-Hudson/Target will settle for 50 percent, Citibank for 75, and Discover for 80, for example.

Negotiating a settlement is a lot like buying a car. Say you're trying to settle out a Citibank account and you know they'll do it at 75 percent. The collector's first offer is going to be 90 percent (because he gets commission on everything he brings in, right?). Your first offer should be 50 percent (even though you know they won't go for it). Eventually you'll both meet somewhere in the middle.

- Issue "state complaints" for every perceived offense. State authorities know that bill collectors break the law occasionally, so each state has a group of agency watchdogs within its commerce or state department. The important thing to remember, though, is to call the department of commerce in the state in which the agency is located. Complaints from other state governments really don't mean much, but an agency's home state is the one that issues collection licenses.

  Some agencies will fire a collector after he gets one or two state complaints, some after ten or twelve, but every collector will get disappeared if he accumulates enough. The agency just can't take the chance that they'll get a whopping fine for his continued aggression.

- If they sue you, make them prove everything. The agency's attorney is expecting to just sign the papers and send them to your local courthouse to get a judgment by default (that is, he's expecting you won't show up for your court date). That's how they make their money—by hoping you'll be too ashamed to take advantage of your day in court. Don't let them win that easily. What you want to do is file a "writ of denial," a legal form that basically means you deny the whole thing. Because most agencies aren't willing to send their attorney (who may know little or nothing about your case) to your local courthouse, which could be a thousand miles away, it's quite possible that they'll just drop the whole thing.

- Know the FDCPA inside and out. Knowledge is your best defense against abuse of power. Even mentioning the name of the legislation will make your collector pause and force him to change his strategy. In addition to parts of the act that I've already mentioned, the following things are illegal under the FDCPA:

> Contacting you before 8 A.M. or after 9 P.M., your time, is prohibited unless a collector has reason to believe that other hours are less convenient for you.
> Contacting you at work is prohibited if the collector has reason to believe that you're not allowed to get calls at work.
> A collector may not discuss your bill with anyone other than yourself or your spouse.
> A collector cannot cause the phone to ring or engage any person (including you) in conversation repeatedly with intent to annoy, abuse, or harass said person.
> A collector cannot use obscene or profane language or lie in any way.

- Some people, including myself, would say that the best way to beat the bill collector is by not letting him find you in the first place. Use your new-found knowledge of skiptracing techniques to avoid being found. Remember, they can't sue what they can't find.

Beating the bill collector is in many ways a waiting game. To them, you're just another slimy debtor who's trying to run out on what he owes. They may spend two and a half minutes thinking about you, at most, each day.

To you, they're a major source of strife in your life. You may think about them all day long, plotting strategy and lying in wait for them to make an illegal mistake. In a scenario like this, the odds are that you'll win.

Getting you to pay means just another step toward goal for a collector. Getting them off your back means a savings of hundreds of dollars to you. Winning for them means getting you to send money you can ill afford to lose. Winning for you means they give up and go off in

41

search of easier prey. You have the motive and opportunity to win, and using the information in this book, you probably will. Don't let the bastards grind you down.

Appendix A:
The Fair Debt Collections Practices Act

OK, don't take my word for it. Here's a copy of the FDCPA, as passed by Congress:

15 USC Sec. 1692
TITLE 15—COMMERCE AND TRADE
CHAPTER 41—CONSUMER CREDIT PROTECTION
SUBCHAPTER V—DEBT COLLECTION PRACTICES

Sec. 1692. Congressional findings and declaration of purpose

-STATUTE-

(a) Abusive practices

There is abundant evidence of the use of abusive, deceptive, and unfair debt collection practices by many debt collectors. Abusive debt collection practices contribute to the number of personal bankruptcies, to marital instability, to the loss of jobs, and to invasions of individual privacy.

(b) Inadequacy of laws

Existing laws and procedures for redressing these injuries are inadequate to protect consumers.

(c) Available non-abusive collection methods

Means other than misrepresentation or other abusive debt collection practices are available for the effective collection of debts.

(d) Interstate commerce

Abusive debt collection practices are carried on to a substantial extent in interstate commerce and through means and instrumentalities of such commerce. Even where abusive debt collection practices are purely intrastate in character, they nevertheless directly affect interstate commerce.

(e) Purposes

It is the purpose of this subchapter to eliminate abusive debt collection practices by debt collectors, to insure that those debt collectors who refrain from using abusive debt collection practices are not competitively disadvantaged, and to promote consistent State action to protect consumers against debt collection abuses.

EFFECTIVE DATE

Section 818 of title VIII of Pub. L. 90-321, as added Pub. L.95-109, provided that:
"This title (enacting this subchapter)
takes effect upon the expiration of six months after the date of its enactment (Sept. 20, 1977), but section 809 (section 1692g of this title) shall apply only with respect to debts for which the initial attempt to collect occurs after such effective date."

SHORT TITLE

This subchapter known as the "Fair Debt Collection Practices Act", see Short Title note set out under section 1601 of this title.

TITLE 15—COMMERCE AND TRADE
CHAPTER 41—CONSUMER CREDIT PROTECTION
SUBCHAPTER V—DEBT COLLECTION PRACTICES

Sec. 1692a. Definitions

-STATUTE-

As used in this subchapter -

(1) The term "Commission" means the Federal Trade Commission.

(2) The term "communication" means the conveying of information regarding a debt directly or indirectly to any person through any medium.

(3) The term "consumer" means any natural person obligated or allegedly obligated to pay any debt.

(4) The term "creditor" means any person who offers or extends credit creating a debt or to whom a debt is owed, but such term does not include any person to the extent that he receives an assignment or transfer of a debt in default solely for the purpose of facilitating collection of such debt for another.

(5) The term "debt" means any obligation or alleged obligation of a consumer to pay money arising out of a transaction in which the money, property, insurance, or services which are the subject of the transaction are primarily for personal, family, or household purposes, whether or not such obligation has been reduced to judgment.

(6) The term "debt collector" means any person who uses any instrumentality of interstate commerce or the mails in any business the principal purpose of which is the collection of any debts, or who regularly collects or attempts to collect, directly or indirectly, debts owed or due or asserted to be owed or due another. Notwithstanding the exclusion provided by clause (F) of the last

sentence of this paragraph, the term includes any creditor who, in the process of collecting his own debts, uses any name other than his own which would indicate that a third person is collecting or attempting to collect such debts. For the purpose of section 1692f(6) of this title, such term also includes any person who uses any instrumentality of interstate commerce or the mails in any business the principal purpose of which is the enforcement of security interests. The term does not include -

(A) any officer or employee of a creditor while, in the name of the creditor, collecting debts for such creditor;

(B) any person while acting as a debt collector for another person, both of whom are related by common ownership or affiliated by corporate control, if the person acting as a debt collector does so only for persons to whom it is so related or affiliated and if the principal business of such person is not the collection of debts;

(C) any officer or employee of the United States or any State to the extent that collecting or attempting to collect any debt is in the performance of his official duties;

(D) any person while serving or attempting to serve legal process on any other person in connection with the judicial enforcement of any debt;

(E) any nonprofit organization which, at the request of consumers, performs bona fide consumer credit counseling and assists consumers in the liquidation of their debts by receiving payments from such consumers and distributing such amounts to creditors; and

(F) any person collecting or attempting to collect any debt owed or due or asserted to be owed or due another to the extent such activity (i) is incidental to a bona fide fiduciary obligation or a bona fide escrow arrangement; (ii) concerns a debt which was originated by such person; (iii) concerns a debt which was not in default at the time it was obtained by such person; or (iv) concerns a debt obtained by such person as a secured party in a commercial credit transaction involving the creditor.

(7) The term "location information" means a consumer's place of abode and his telephone number at such place, or his place of employment.

(8) The term "State" means any State, territory, or possession of the United States, the District of Columbia, the Commonwealth of Puerto Rico, or any political subdivision of any of the foregoing.

-SOURCE-

(Pub. L. 90-321, title VIII, Sec. 803, as added Pub. L. 95-109, Sept. 20, 1977, 91 Stat. 875; amended Pub. L. 99-361, July 9, 1986, 100 Stat. 768.)

AMENDMENTS

1986—Par. (6). Pub. L. 99-361 in provision preceding cl. (A) substituted "clause (F)" for "clause (G)", struck out cl. (F) which excluded any attorney-at-law collecting a debt as an attorney on behalf of and in the name of a client from term "debt collector", and redesignated cl. (G) as (F).

TITLE 15—COMMERCE AND TRADE
CHAPTER 41—CONSUMER CREDIT PROTECTION
SUBCHAPTER V—DEBT COLLECTION PRACTICES

Sec. 1692b. Acquisition of location information

-STATUTE-

Any debt collector communicating with any person other than the consumer for the purpose of acquiring location information about the consumer shall—(1) identify himself, state that he is confirming or correcting location information concerning the consumer, and, only if expressly requested, identify his employer; (2) r.ot state that such consumer owes any debt; (3) not communicate with any such person more than once unless requested to do so by such person or unless the debt collector reasonably believes that the earlier response of such person is erroneous or incom-

plete and that such person now has correct or complete location information; (4) not communicate by post card; (5) not use any language or symbol on any envelope or in the contents of any communication effected by the mails or telegram that indicates that the debt collector is in the debt collection business or that the communication relates to the collection of a debt; and (6) after the debt collector knows the consumer is represented by an attorney with regard to the subject debt and has knowledg of, or can readily ascertain, such attorney's name and address, not communicate with any person other than that attorney, unless the attorney fails to respond within a reasonable period of time
to communication from the debt collector.

-SOURCE-

(Pub. L. 90-321, title VIII, Sec. 804, as added Pub. L. 95-109, Sept. 20, 1977, 91 Stat. 876.)

TITLE 15—COMMERCE AND TRADE
CHAPTER 41—CONSUMER CREDIT PROTECTION
SUBCHAPTER V—DEBT COLLECTION PRACTICES

Sec. 1692c. Communication in connection with debt collection

-STATUTE-

(a) Communication with the consumer generally

Without the prior consent of the consumer given directly to the debt collector or the express permission of a court of competent jurisdiction, a debt collector may not communicate with a consumer in connection with the collection of any debt—(1) at any unusual time or place or a time or place known or which should be known to be inconvenient to the consumer. In the absence of knowledge of circumstances to the contrary, a debt collector shall assume that the convenient time for communicating with a consumer is after 8 o'clock antemeridian and before 9 o'clock postmeridian, local time at the consumer's location; (2) if the debt collector knows the consumer is represented by an attorney with respect to such debt and has knowledge of, or can readily ascertain, such attorney's name and address, unless the attorney fails to respond within a reasonable period of time to a communication from the debt collector or unless the attorney consents to direct communication with the consumer; or (3) at the consumer's place of employment if the debt collector knows or has reason to know that the consumer's employer prohibits the consumer from receiving such communication.

(b) Communication with third parties

Except as provided in section 1692b of this title, without the prior consent of the consumer given directly to the debt collector, or the express permission of a court of competent jurisdiction, or as reasonably necessary to effectuate a postjudgment judicial remedy, a debt collector may not communicate, in connection with the collection of any debt, with any person other than the consumer, his attorney, a consumer reporting agency if otherwise permitted by law, the creditor, the attorney of the creditor, or the attorney of the debt collector.

(c) Ceasing communication

If a consumer notifies a debt collector in writing that the consumer refuses to pay a debt or that the consumer wishes the debt collector to cease further communication with the consumer, the debt collector shall not communicate further with the consumer with respect to such debt, except—(1) to advise the consumer that the debt collector's further efforts are being terminated; (2) to notify the consumer that the debt collector or creditor may invoke specified remedies which are ordinarily invoked by such debt collector or creditor; or (3) where applicable, to notify the consumer that the debt collector or creditor intends to invoke a specified remedy. If such notice from the consumer is made by mail, notification shall be complete upon receipt.

(d) "Consumer" defined

For the purpose of this section, the term "consumer" includes the consumer's spouse, parent (if the consumer is a minor), guardian, executor, or administrator.

-SOURCE-

(Pub. L. 90-321, title VIII, Sec. 805, as added Pub. L. 95-109, Sept. 20, 1977, 91 Stat. 876.)

TITLE 15—COMMERCE AND TRADE
CHAPTER 41—CONSUMER CREDIT PROTECTION
SUBCHAPTER V—DEBT COLLECTION PRACTICES

Sec. 1692d. Harassment or abuse

-STATUTE-

A debt collector may not engage in any conduct the natural consequence of which is to harass, oppress, or abuse any person in connection with the collection of a debt. Without limiting the general application of the foregoing, the following conduct is a violation of this section:

(1) The use or threat of use of violence or other criminal means to harm the physical person, reputation, or property of any person.

(2) The use of obscene or profane language or language the natural consequence of which is to abuse the hearer or reader.

(3) The publication of a list of consumers who allegedly refuse to pay debts, except to a consumer reporting agency or to persons meeting the requirements of section 1681a(f) or 1681b(3) of this title.

(4) The advertisement for sale of any debt to coerce payment of the debt.

(5) Causing a telephone to ring or engaging any person in telephone conversation repeatedly or continuously with intent to annoy, abuse, or harass any person at the called number.

(6) Except as provided in section 1692b of this title, the placement of telephone calls without meaningful disclosure of the caller's identity.

-SOURCE-

(Pub. L. 90-321, title VIII, Sec. 806, as added Pub. L. 95-109, Sept. 20, 1977, 91 Stat. 877.)

TITLE 15—COMMERCE AND TRADE
CHAPTER 41—CONSUMER CREDIT PROTECTION
SUBCHAPTER V—DEBT COLLECTION PRACTICES

Sec. 1692e. False or misleading representations

-STATUTE-

A debt collector may not use any false, deceptive, or misleading representation or means in connection with the collection of any debt. Without limiting the general application of the foregoing, the following conduct is a violation of this section:

(1) The false representation or implication that the debt collector is vouched for, bonded by, or affiliated with the United States or any State, including the use of any badge, uniform, or facsimile thereof.

(2) The false representation of -

(A) the character, amount, or legal status of any debt; or

(B) any services rendered or compensation which may be lawfully received by any debt collector for the collection of a debt.

(3) The false representation or implication that any individual is an attorney or that any communication is from an attorney.

(4) The representation or implication that nonpayment of any debt will result in the arrest or imprisonment of any person or the seizure, garnishment, attachment, or sale of any property or wages of any person unless such action is lawful and the debt collector or creditor intends to take such action.

(5) The threat to take any action that cannot legally be take or that is not intended to be taken.

(6) The false representation or implication that a sale, referral, or other transfer of any interest in a debt shall cause the consumer to-

(A) lose any claim or defense to payment of the debt; or

(B) become subject to any practice prohibited by this subchapter.

(7) The false representation or implication that the consumer committed any crime or other conduct in order to disgrace the consumer.

(8) Communicating or threatening to communicate to any person credit information which is known or which should be known to be false, including the failure to communicate that a disputed debt is disputed.

(9) The use or distribution of any written communication which simulates or is falsely represented to be a document authorized, issued, or approved by any court, official, or agency of the United States or any State, or which creates a false impression as to its source, authorization, or approval.

(10) The use of any false representation or deceptive means to collect or attempt to collect any debt or to obtain information concerning a consumer.

(11) Except as otherwise provided for communications to acquire location information under section 1692b of this title, the failure to disclose clearly in all communications made to collect a debt or to obtain information about a consumer, that the debt collector is attempting to collect a debt and that any information obtained will be used for that purpose.

(12) The false representation or implication that accounts have been turned over to innocent purchasers for value.

(13) The false representation or implication that documents are legal process.

(14) The use of any business, company, or organization name other than the true name of the debt collector's business, company, or organization.

(15) The false representation or implication that documents are not legal process forms or do not require action by the consumer.

(16) The false representation or implication that a debt collector operates or is employed by a consumer reporting agency as defined by section 1681a(f) of this title.

-SOURCE-

(Pub. L. 90-321, title VIII, Sec. 807, as added Pub. L. 95-109, Sept. 20, 1977, 91 Stat. 877.)

TITLE 15—COMMERCE AND TRADE
CHAPTER 41—CONSUMER CREDIT PROTECTION
SUBCHAPTER V—DEBT COLLECTION PRACTICES

Sec. 1692f. Unfair practices

-STATUTE-

A debt collector may not use unfair or unconscionable means to collect or attempt to collect any debt. Without limiting the general application of the foregoing, the following conduct is a violation of this section:

(1) The collection of any amount (including any interest, fee, charge, or expense incidental to the principal obligation) unless such amount is expressly authorized by the agreement creating the debt or permitted by law.

(2) The acceptance by a debt collector from any person of a check or other payment instrument postdated by more than five days unless such person is notified in writing of the debt collector's intent to deposit such check or instrument not more than ten nor less than three business days prior to such deposit.

(3) The solicitation by a debt collector of any postdated check or other postdated payment instrument for the purpose of threatening or instituting criminal prosecution.

(4) Depositing or threatening to deposit any postdated check or other postdated payment instrument prior to the date on such check or instrument.

(5) Causing charges to be made to any person for communications by concealment of the true purpose of the communication. Such charges include, but are not limited to, collect telephone calls and telegram fees.

(6) Taking or threatening to take any nonjudicial action to effect dispossession or disablement of property if -

(A) there is no present right to possession of the property claimed as collateral through an enforceable security interest;

(B) there is no present intention to take possession of the property; or

(C) the property is exempt by law from such dispossession or disablement.

(7) Communicating with a consumer regarding a debt by postcard.

(8) Using any language or symbol, other than the debt collector's address, on any envelope when communicating with a consumer by use of the mails or by telegram, except that a debt collector may use his business name if such name does not indicate that he is in the debt collection business.

-SOURCE-

(Pub. L. 90-321, title VIII, Sec. 808, as added Pub. L. 95-109, Sept. 20, 1977, 91 Stat. 879.)

TITLE 15—COMMERCE AND TRADE
CHAPTER 41—CONSUMER CREDIT PROTECTION
SUBCHAPTER V—DEBT COLLECTION PRACTICES

Sec. 1692g. Validation of debts

-STATUTE-

(a) Notice of debt; contents

Within five days after the initial communication with a consumer in connection with the collection of any debt, a debt collector shall, unless the following information is contained in the initial communication or the consumer has paid the debt, send the consumer a written notice containing -

(1) the amount of the debt;

(2) the name of the creditor to whom the debt is owed;

(3) a statement that unless the consumer, within thirty days after receipt of the notice, disputes the validity of the debt, or any portion thereof, the debt will be assumed to be valid by the debt collector;

(4) a statement that if the consumer notifies the debt collector in writing within the thirty-day period that the debt, or any portion thereof, is disputed, the debt collector will obtain verification of the debt or a copy of a judgment against the consumer and a copy of such verification or judgment will be mailed to the consumer by the debt collector; and

(5) a statement that, upon the consumer's written request within the thirty-day period, the debt collector will provide the consumer with the name and address of the original creditor, if different from the current creditor.

(b) Disputed debts

If the consumer notifies the debt collector in writing within the thirty-day period described in subsection (a) of this section that the debt, or any portion thereof, is disputed, or that the consumer requests the name and address of the original creditor, the debt collector shall cease collection of the debt, or any disputed portion thereof, until the debt collector obtains verification of the debt or a copy of a judgment, or the name and address of the original creditor, and a copy of such verification or judgment, or name and address of the original creditor, is mailed to the consumer by the debt collector.

(c) Admission of liability

The failure of a consumer to dispute the validity of a debt under this section may not be construed by any court as an admission of liability by the consumer.

-SOURCE-

(Pub. L. 90-321, title VIII, Sec. 809, as added Pub. L. 95-109, Sept. 20, 1977, 91 Stat. 879.)

EFFECTIVE DATE

Section applicable only with respect to debts for which the initial attempt to collect occurs after the effective date of this subchapter, which takes effect upon the expiration of six months after Sept. 20, 1977, see section 818 of Pub. L. 90-321, set out as a note under section 1692 of this title.

TITLE 15—COMMERCE AND TRADE
CHAPTER 41—CONSUMER CREDIT PROTECTION
SUBCHAPTER V—DEBT COLLECTION PRACTICES

Sec. 1692h. Multiple debts

-STATUTE-

If any consumer owes multiple debts and makes any single payment to any debt collector with respect to such debts, such debt collector may not apply such payment to any debt which is disputed by the consumer and, where applicable, shall apply such payment in accordance with the consumer's directions.

-SOURCE-

(Pub. L. 90-321, title VIII, Sec. 810, as added Pub. L. 95-109, Sept. 20, 1977, 91 Stat. 880.)

TITLE 15—COMMERCE AND TRADE
CHAPTER 41—CONSUMER CREDIT PROTECTION
SUBCHAPTER V—DEBT COLLECTION PRACTICES

Sec. 1692i. Legal actions by debt collectors

-STATUTE-

(a) Venue

Any debt collector who brings any legal action on a debt against any consumer shall -

(1) in the case of an action to enforce an interest in real property securing the consumer's obligation, bring such action only in a judicial district or similar legal entity in which such real property is located; or

(2) in the case of an action not described in paragraph (1), bring such action only in the judicial district or similar legal entity -

(A) in which such consumer signed the contract sued upon; or

(B) in which such consumer resides at the commencement of the action.

(b) Authorization of actions

Nothing in this subchapter shall be construed to authorize the bringing of legal actions by debt collectors.

-SOURCE-

(Pub. L. 90-321, title VIII, Sec. 811, as added Pub. L. 95-109, Sept. 20, 1977, 91 Stat. 880.

TITLE 15—COMMERCE AND TRADE
CHAPTER 41—CONSUMER CREDIT PROTECTION
SUBCHAPTER V—DEBT COLLECTION PRACTICES

Sec. 1692j. Furnishing certain deceptive forms

-STATUTE-

(a) It is unlawful to design, compile, and furnish any form knowing that such form would be used to create the false belief in a consumer that a person other than the creditor of such consumer is participating in the collection of or in an attempt to collect a debt such consumer allegedly owes such creditor, when in fact such person is not so participating.

(b) Any person who violates this section shall be liable to the same extent and in the same manner as a debt collector is liable under section 1692k of this title for failure to comply with a provision of this subchapter.

-SOURCE-

(Pub. L. 90-321, title VIII, Sec. 812, as added Pub. L. 95-109, Sept. 20, 1977, 91 Stat. 880.)

TITLE 15—COMMERCE AND TRADE
CHAPTER 41—CONSUMER CREDIT PROTECTION
SUBCHAPTER V—DEBT COLLECTION PRACTICES

Sec. 1692k. Civil liability

-STATUTE-

(a) Amount of damages

Except as otherwise provided by this section, any debt collector who fails to comply with any provision of this subchapter with respect to any person is liable to such person in an amount equal to the sum of -

(1) any actual damage sustained by such person as a result of such failure;

(2)(A) in the case of any action by an individual, such additional damages as the court may allow, but not exceeding $1,000; or

(B) in the case of a class action, (i) such amount for each named plaintiff as could be recovered under subparagraph (A), and (ii) such amount as the court may allow for all other class members, without regard to a minimum individual recovery, not to exceed the lesser of $500,000 or 1 per centum of the net worth of the debt collector; and

(3) in the case of any successful action to enforce the foregoing liability, the costs of the action, together with a reasonable attorney's fee as determined by the court. On a finding by the court that an action under this section was brought in bad faith and for the purpose of harassment, the court may award to the defendant attorney's fees reasonable in relation to the work expended and costs.

(b) Factors considered by court

In determining the amount of liability in any action under subsection (a) of this section, the court shall consider, among other relevant factors -

(1) in any individual action under subsection (a)(2)(A) of this section, the frequency and persistence of noncompliance by the debt collector, the nature of such noncompliance, and the extent to which such noncompliance was intentional; or

(2) in any class action under subsection (a)(2)(B) of this section, the frequency and persistence of noncompliance by the debt collector, the nature of such noncompliance, the resources of the debt collector, the number of persons adversely affected, and the extent to which the debt collector's noncompliance was intentional.

(c) Intent

A debt collector may not be held liable in any action brought under this subchapter if the debt collector shows by a preponderance of evidence that the violation was not intentional and resulted from a bona fide error notwithstanding the maintenance of procedures reasonably adapted to avoid any such error.

(d) Jurisdiction

An action to enforce any liability created by this subchapter may be brought in any appropriate United States district court without regard to the amount in controversy, or in any other court of competent jurisdiction, within one year from the date on which the violation occurs.

(e) Advisory opinions of Commission

No provision of this section imposing any liability shall apply to any act done or omitted in good faith in conformity with any advisory opinion of the Commission, notwithstanding that after such act or omission has occurred, such opinion is amended, rescinded, or determined by judicial or other authority to be invalid for any reason.

-SOURCE-
(Pub. L. 90-321, title VIII, Sec. 813, as added Pub. L. 95-109, Sept. 20, 1977, 91 Stat. 881.)

TITLE 15—COMMERCE AND TRADE
CHAPTER 41—CONSUMER CREDIT PROTECTION
SUBCHAPTER V—DEBT COLLECTION PRACTICES

Sec. 1692l. Administrative enforcement

-STATUTE-

(a) Federal Trade Commission

Compliance with this subchapter shall be enforced by the Commission, except to the extent that enforcement of the requirements imposed under this subchapter is specifically committed to another agency under subsection (b) of this section. For purpose of the exercise by the Commission of its functions and powers under the Federal Trade Commission Act (15 U.S.C. 41 et seq.), a violation of this subchapter shall be deemed an unfair or deceptive act or practice in violation of that Act. All of the functions and powers of the Commission under the Federal Trade Commission Act are available to the Commission to enforce compliance by any person with this subchapter, irrespective of whether that person is engaged in commerce or meets any other jurisdictional tests in the Federal Trade Commission Act, including the power to enforce the provisions of this subchapter in the same manner as if the violation had been a violation of a Federal Trade Commission trade regulation rule.

(b) Applicable provisions of law

Compliance with any requirements imposed under this subchapter shall be enforced under -

(1) section 8 of the Federal Deposit Insurance Act (12 U.S.C. 1818), in the case of
(A) national banks, and Federal branches and Federal agencies of foreign banks, by the Office of the Comptroller of the Currency;

(B) member banks of the Federal Reserve System (other than national banks), branches and agencies of foreign banks (other than Federal branches, Federal agencies, and insured State branches of foreign banks), commercial lending companies owned or controlled by foreign banks, and organizations operating under section 25 or 25(a) (FOOTNOTE 1) of the Federal Reserve Act (12 U.S.C. 601 et seq., 611 et seq.), by the Board of Governors of the Federal Reserve System; and (FOOTNOTE 1) See References in Text note below.

(C) banks insured by the Federal Deposit Insurance Corporation (other than members of the Federal Reserve System) and insured State branches of foreign banks, by the Board of Directors of the Federal Deposit Insurance Corporation;

(2) section 8 of the Federal Deposit Insurance Act (12 U.S.C. 1818), by the Director of the Office of Thrift Supervision, in the case of a savings association the deposits of which are insured by the Federal Deposit Insurance Corporation;

(3) the Federal Credit Union Act (12 U.S.C. 1751 et seq.), by the National Credit Union Administration Board with respect to any Federal credit union;

(4) subtitle IV of title 49, by the Secretary of Transportation, with respect to all carriers subject to the jurisdiction of the Surface Transportation Board;

(5) part A of subtitle VII of title 49, by the Secretary of Transportation with respect to any air carrier or any foreign air carrier subject to that part; and

(6) the Packers and Stockyards Act, 1921 (7 U.S.C. 181 et seq.) (except as provided in section 406 of that Act (7 U.S.C. 226, 227)), by the Secretary of Agriculture with respect to any activities subject to that Act.

The terms used in paragraph (1) that are not defined in this subchapter or otherwise defined in section 3(s) of the Federal Deposit Insurance Act (12 U.S.C. 1813(s)) shall have the meaning given to them in section 1(b) of the International Banking Act of 1978 (12 U.S.C. 3101).

(c) Agency powers

For the purpose of the exercise by any agency referred to in subsection (b) of this section of its powers under any Act referred to in that subsection, a violation of any requirement imposed under this subchapter shall be deemed to be a violation of a requirement imposed under that Act. In addition to its powers under any provision of law specifically referred to in subsection (b) of this section, each of the agencies referred to in that subsection may exercise, for the purpose of enforcing compliance with any requirement imposed under this subchapter any other authority conferred on it by law, except as provided in subsection (d) of this section.

(d) Rules and regulations

Neither the Commission nor any other agency referred to in subsection (b) of this section may promulgate trade regulation rules or other regulations with respect to the collection of debts by debt collectors as defined in this subchapter.

-SOURCE-

(Pub. L. 90-321, title VIII, Sec. 814, as added Pub. L. 95-109, Sept. 20, 1977, 91 Stat. 881; amended Pub. L. 95-630, title V, Sec. 501, Nov. 10, 1978, 92 Stat. 3680; Pub. L. 98-443, Sec. 9(n), Oct. 4, 1984, 98 Stat. 1708; Pub. L. 101-73, title VII, Sec. 744(n), Aug. 9, 1989, 103 Stat. 440; Pub. L. 102-242, title II, Sec. 212(e), Dec. 19, 1991, 105 Stat. 2301; Pub. L. 102-550, title XVI, Sec. 1604(a)(8), Oct. 28, 1992, 106 Stat. 4082; Pub. L. 104-88, title III, Sec. 316, Dec. 29, 1995, 109 Stat. 949.)

REFERENCES IN TEXT

The Federal Trade Commission Act, referred to in subsec. (a), is act Sept. 26, 1914, ch. 311, 38 Stat. 717, as amended, which is classified generally to subchapter I (Sec. 41 et seq.) of chapter 2 of this title. For complete classification of this Act to the Code, see section 58 of this title and Tables. Section 25(a) of the Federal Reserve Act, referred to in subsec. (b)(1)(B), which is classified to subchapter II (Sec. 611 et seq.)of chapter 6 of Title 12, Banks and Banking, was renumbered section 25A of that act by Pub. L. 102-242, title I, Sec. 142(e)(2), Dec. 19, 1991, 105 Stat. 2281. Section 25 of the Federal Reserve Act is classified to subchapter I (Sec. 601 et seq.) of chapter 6 of Title 12. The Federal Credit Union Act, referred to in subsec. (b)(3), is act June 26, 1934, ch. 750, 48 Stat. 1216, as amended, which is classified generally to chapter 14 (Sec. 1751 et seq.) of Title 12. For complete classification of this Act to the Code, see section 1751 of Title 12 and Tables.

The Packers and Stockyards Act, 1921, referred to in subsec. (b)(6), is act Aug. 15, 1921, ch. 64, 42 Stat. 159, as amended, which is classified generally to chapter 9 (Sec. 181 et seq.) of Title 7, Agriculture. For complete classification of this Act to the Code, see section 181 of Title 7 and Tables.

CODIFICATION

In subsec. (b)(4), "subtitle IV of title 49" substituted for "the Acts to regulate commerce" on authority of Pub. L. 95-473, Sec. 3(b), Oct. 17, 1978, 92 Stat. 1466, the first section of which enacted subtitle IV of Title 49, Transportation.

In subsec. (b)(5), "part A of subtitle VII of title 49" substituted for "the Federal Aviation Act of 1958 (49 App. U.S.C. 1301 et seq.)" and "that part" substituted for "that Act" on authority of Pub. L. 103-272, Sec. 6(b), July 5, 1994, 108 Stat. 1378, the first section of which enacted subtitles II, III, and V to X of Title 49.

AMENDMENTS

1995—Subsec. (b)(4). Pub. L. 104-88 substituted "Secretary of Transportation, with respect to all carriers subject to the jurisdiction of the Surface Transportation Board" for "Interstate Commerce Commission with respect to any common carrier subject to those Acts".

1992—Subsec. (b)(1)(C). Pub. L. 102-550 substituted semicolon for period at end.

1991—Subsec. (b). Pub. L. 102-242, Sec. 212(e)(2), inserted at end "The terms used in paragraph (1) that are not defined in this subchapter or otherwise defined in section 3(s) of the Federal Deposit Insurance Act (12 U.S.C. 1813(s)) shall have the meaning given to them in section 1(b) of the International Banking Act of 1978 (12 U.S.C. 3101)."

Pub. L. 102-242, Sec. 212(e)(1), added par. (1) and struck out former par. (1) which read as follows: "section 8 of Federal Deposit Insurance Act, in the case of -

"(A) national banks, by the Comptroller of the Currency;

"(B) member banks of the Federal Reserve System (other than national banks), by the Federal Reserve Board; and

"(C) banks the deposits or accounts of which are insured by the Federal Deposit Insurance Corporation (other than members of the Federal Reserve System), by the Board of Directors of the Federal Deposit Insurance Corporation;".

1989—Subsec. (b)(2). Pub. L. 101-73 amended par. (2) generally. Prior to amendment, par. (2) read as follows: "section 5(d) of the Home Owners Loan Act of 1933, section 407 of the National Housing Act, and sections 6(i) and 17 of the Federal Home Loan Bank Act, by the Federal Home Loan Bank Board (acting directly or through the Federal Savings and Loan Insurance Corporation), in the case of any institution subject to any of those provisions;".

1984—Subsec. (b)(5). Pub. L. 98-443 substituted "Secretary of Transportation" for "Civil Aeronautics Board".

EFFECTIVE DATE OF 1995 AMENDMENT

Amendment by Pub. L. 104-88 effective Jan. 1, 1996, see section 2 of Pub. L. 104-88, set out as an Effective Date note under section 701 of Title 49, Transportation.

EFFECTIVE DATE OF 1992 AMENDMENT

Amendment by Pub. L. 102-550 effective as if included in the Federal Deposit Insurance Corporation Improvement Act of 1991, Pub. L. 102-242, as of Dec. 19, 1991, see section 1609(a) of Pub. L. 102-550, set out as a note under section 191 of Title 12, Banks and Banking.

EFFECTIVE DATE OF 1984 AMENDMENT

Amendment by Pub. L. 98-443 effective Jan. 1, 1985, see section 9(v) of Pub. L. 98-443, set out as a note under section 5314 of Title 5, Government Organization and Employees.

TRANSFER OF FUNCTIONS

''National Credit Union Administration Board'' substituted for ''Administrator of the National Credit Union Administration'' in subsec. (b)(3) pursuant to section 501 of Pub. L. 95-630 (12 U.S.C. 1752a) which vested authority for management of National Credit Union Administration in National Credit Union Administration Board.

SECTION REFERRED TO IN OTHER SECTIONS

This section is referred to in section 1692m of this title

TITLE 15—COMMERCE AND TRADE
CHAPTER 41—CONSUMER CREDIT PROTECTION
SUBCHAPTER V—DEBT COLLECTION PRACTICES

Sec. 1692m. Reports to Congress by the Commission; views of other Federal agencies

-STATUTE-

(a) Not later than one year after the effective date of this subchapter and at one-year intervals thereafter, the Commission shall make reports to the Congress concerning the administration of its functions under this subchapter, including such recommendations as the Commission deems necessary or appropriate. In addition, each report of the Commission shall include its assessment of the extent to which compliance with this subchapter is being achieved and a summary of the enforcement actions taken by the Commission under section 1692l of this title.

(b) In the exercise of its functions under this subchapter, the Commission may obtain upon request the views of any other Federal agency which exercises enforcement functions under section 1692l of this title.

-SOURCE-

(Pub. L. 90-321, title VIII, Sec. 815, as added Pub. L. 95-109, Sept. 20, 1977, 91 Stat. 882.)

REFERENCES IN TEXT

The effective date of this subchapter, referred to in subsec. (a), is the date occurring on expiration of six months after Sept. 20, 1977. See section 818 of Pub. L. 90-321, set out as an Effective Date note under section 1692 of this title.

TITLE 15—COMMERCE AND TRADE
CHAPTER 41—CONSUMER CREDIT PROTECTION
SUBCHAPTER V—DEBT COLLECTION PRACTICES

Sec. 1692n. Relation to State laws

-STATUTE-

This subchapter does not annul, alter, or affect, or exempt any person subject to the provisions of this subchapter from complying with the laws of any State with respect to debt collection practices, except to the extent that those laws are inconsistent with any provision of this subchapter, and then only to the extent of the inconsistency. For purposes of this section, a State law is not inconsistent with this subchapter if the protection such law affords any consumer is greater than the protection provided by this subchapter.

-SOURCE-

(Pub. L. 90-321, title VIII, Sec. 816, as added Pub. L. 95-109, Sept. 20, 1977, 91 Stat. 883.)

TITLE 15—COMMERCE AND TRADE
CHAPTER 41—CONSUMER CREDIT PROTECTION
SUBCHAPTER V—DEBT COLLECTION PRACTICES

Sec. 1692o. Exemption for State regulation

-STATUTE-

The Commission shall by regulation exempt from the requirements of this subchapter any class of debt collection practices within any State if the Commission determines that under the law of that State that class of debt collection practices is subject to requirements substantially similar to those imposed by this subchapter, and that there is adequate provision for enforcement.

-SOURCE-

(Pub. L. 90-321, title VIII, Sec. 817, as added Pub. L. 95-109, Sept. 20, 1977, 91 Stat. 883.)